D0556847

COLD SASSY TREE

Olive Ann Burns

TECHNICAL DIRECTOR Maxwell Krohn
EDITORIAL DIRECTOR Justin Kestler
MANAGING EDITOR Ben Florman

SERIES EDITORS Boomie Aglietti, Justin Kestler
PRODUCTION Christian Lorentzen

WRITERS Brian Phillips, Margaret Marie Tinucci
EDITORS Emma Chastain, Thomas Connors

This edition published by Spark Publishing

Spark Publishing
A Division of SparkNotes LLC
120 Fifth Avenue, 8th Floor
New York, NY 10011

02 03 04 05 SN 9 8 7 6 5 4 3 2 1

Please send all comments and questions or report errors to
feedback@sparknotes.com.

Library of Congress information available upon request

Printed and bound in the United States

RRD-C

ISBN 1-58663-506-9

Introduction:
Stopping to Buy SparkNotes on a Snowy Evening

Whose words these are you *think* you know.
Your paper's due tomorrow, though;
We're glad to see you stopping here
To get some help before you go.

Lost your course? You'll find it here.
Face tests and essays without fear.
Between the words, good grades at stake:
Get great results throughout the year.

Once school bells caused your heart to quake
As teachers circled each mistake.
Use SparkNotes and no longer weep,
Ace every single test you take.

Yes, books are lovely, dark, and deep,
But only what you grasp you keep,
With hours to go before you sleep,
With hours to go before you sleep.

CONTENTS

CONTEXT

OLIVE ANN BURNS WAS BORN in Banks County, Georgia, in 1924. Burns attended the University of North Carolina at Chapel Hill and began a career as a journalist after graduating. Burns worked as a staff writer for the Sunday magazine of the *Atlanta Journal and Constitution* from 1947 to 1957. From 1960 to 1967, she authored an advice column called "Ask Amy" for a local newspaper, using the pseudonym Amy Larkin. After being diagnosed with cancer in 1976, Burns began her first novel, *Cold Sassy Tree*. The novel, which was published in 1984, took almost nine years to complete. Upon its publication, the novel was both a critical and a commercial success. In 1989, Turner Network Television released a film version of *Cold Sassy Tree* starring Faye Dunaway and Neil Patrick Harris.

Of her career and upbringing, Burns once said, "It has been said that growing up in the South and becoming a writer is like spending your life riding in a wagon, seated in a chair that is always facing backwards. I don't face life looking backwards, but I have written about past times and past people." Tales of the past make up *Cold Sassy Tree*, and Burns models these tales on stories from her own life. Although *Cold Sassy Tree* is not a biographical account of Burns's own family, Burns draws upon the colorful history and idiosyncrasies of her father and his family to evoke Georgia at the beginning of the twentieth century. Burns said of the writing of *Cold Sassy Tree*, "What I was after was not just names and dates. I wanted stories and details that would bring the dead to life." Will Tweedy, the protagonist of *Cold Sassy Tree*, bears many things in common with Burns's father, William Arnold Burns. William Arnold Burns was the grandson of the owner of the general store in Commerce, Georgia; Will Tweedy is the grandson of the owner of the general store in Cold Sassy, Georgia. Will Tweedy is fourteen years old in 1906, just as William Burns was. Burns loosely based the character Rucker on her great-grandfather, and she modeled the fictional town Cold Sassy on her hometown, Commerce.

Following the unexpected popularity of *Cold Sassy Tree*, Burns found herself flooded with mail requesting a sequel to the novel. In 1987, Burns underwent a second round of chemotherapy, which led to congestive heart failure and left her bedridden for more than a year. In February 1988, Burns began to dictate the sequel to *Cold Sassy Tree*, which she planned to title *Time, Dirt and Money*. In this second novel, Burns intended to base the story on her parents' life and marriage during the Great Depression. The manuscript was unfinished at the time of her death on July 4, 1990, but the completed chapters, together with Burns's notes, were published in 1992 as *Leaving Cold Sassy*.

PLOT OVERVIEW

O
N JULY 5, 1906, Rucker Blakeslee announces that he intends to marry Miss Love Simpson, a hat-maker at his store who is years younger than he. This news shocks his family, since his wife Mattie Lou died only three weeks earlier. Rucker's daughters, Mary Willis and Loma, worry about what the gossips of Cold Sassy, Georgia, will think of their father's impropriety. Will Tweedy, Rucker's fourteen-year-old grandson and the narrator of the novel, supports his grandfather's marriage. Will thinks Miss Love is nice and pretty, even though she comes from Baltimore and therefore is practically a Yankee. Will thinks that Rucker needs someone to look after him now that Mattie Lou is gone. On the afternoon Rucker announces his engagement, Will sneaks off to go fishing in the country despite the fact that he is supposed to be in mourning for his grandmother. He walks across a high, narrow train trestle and nearly dies when a train speeds toward him. He survives by hurling himself between the tracks so the train passes just overhead without actually touching him. Will becomes a sensation after his near-death experience, and the whole town comes to his house to ask him about the incident. Rucker shocks everyone by arriving with his new bride, Miss Love.

The people of Cold Sassy disapprove of Rucker's hasty marriage, and rumors spread quickly. Will, however, spends a great deal of time at the Blakeslee house and becomes friends with Miss Love. Will soon learns that the marriage is one of convenience and that Rucker and Miss Love sleep in separate rooms. Miss Love tells Will that she married Rucker only because he promised to deed her the house and furniture. For his part, Rucker married Miss Love to save on the cost of a housekeeper. One day, Clayton McAllister, Miss Love's former fiancé from Texas, shows up and tries to persuade Miss Love to leave with him. He kisses her, but Miss Love sends him away contemptuously. Miss Effie Belle Tate, a local gossip, sees the kiss and promptly spreads the news all over town.

Will and some of his friends make a trip into the country to pick up a horse for Miss Love, camping in the mountains along the way. When they return, Will and his father, Hoyt, try to convince Will's mother, Mary Willis, to go on a trip to New York. Rucker has bought the tickets to New York so that Hoyt, who works for

Rucker, can go to purchase new goods for the store. At first Mary Willis refuses to go because she is in mourning, but Will and Hoyt convince her that the trip will do her good. Right after Mary Willis changes her mind, Rucker decides to use the tickets himself to go to New York with Miss Love. Mary Willis is crushed, and her hatred of Miss Love increases. To take his and Mary Willis's mind off the disappointment, Hoyt buys a brand new Cadillac and becomes the first motorcar owner in Cold Sassy history.

Rucker and Miss Love return from New York. They are now flirtatious and affectionate with each other, and Will wonders whether their marriage is becoming more legitimate. Rucker announces that he too has bought a car and intends to begin selling cars in Cold Sassy. Lightfoot McLendon is a classmate of Will's who lives in the impoverished section of Cold Sassy known as Mill Town. One day Will takes Lightfoot on a car ride to the cemetery, where he kisses her. A nosy neighbor sees the kiss and tells Will's parents. Outraged at Will's association with common people, Will's parents forbid him to drive the Cadillac for two months. Will gets around his punishment by driving Rucker's car. One Sunday, Will, Rucker, and Miss Love take a day trip into the country, where Will gives them driving lessons. On the way back to Cold Sassy, Will crashes the car into a creek bed and damages the radiator. While they wait for a repair team to arrive, they stay with a family that lives nearby. That night, Will overhears Rucker tell Miss Love that he loves her and wants their marriage to be real. Miss Love declares that she cannot marry and that no man would want her if he knew her terrible secret. She tells Rucker that her father raped her when she was a child. Rucker says her past does not lessen his love for her, but Miss Love sends him away.

Eventually, Miss Love and Rucker fall deeply in love. Will's uncle, Camp Williams, commits suicide, which begins a dark period in Cold Sassy. Rucker hires Will's worst enemy, Hosie Roach, to work at the store in Camp's place. Because of his new income, Hosie can marry Will's beloved Lightfoot. A pair of thieves robs and beats Rucker. Although he recovers from his injuries, Rucker catches pneumonia. As Rucker lies sick in bed, Will overhears him tell Miss Love that God provides strength and comfort to the faithful in times of trouble. Miss Love tells Will that although Rucker does not know it, she is pregnant with Rucker's child. Rucker dies shortly after he falls ill, but his message of faith in God gives Will strength to cope. Though the town and Will's family do not accept Miss Love, she knows that they will all accept her child, and plans on staying in Cold Sassy.

CHARACTER LIST

Will Tweedy The novel's narrator and protagonist. Will is a
fourteen-year-old boy growing up Cold Sassy, Georgia
at the very beginning of the twentieth century.
Although he comes from a conventional family, Will is
a free spirit and often feels compelled to defy the rules
governing his life. Following his grandmother's death
and his grandfather's second marriage, Will begins to
grapple with issues of love and death, and his
perspective on life begins to change.

Rucker Blakeslee Will's maternal grandfather. Rucker is a brash,
humorous, and domineering man who owns the
general store in Cold Sassy. Rucker is passionately
Southern, but he has no use for the gossip and
hypocrisy of Cold Sassy's small-town ways, and he
acts according to his own code of decent conduct, not
the town's.

Miss Love Simpson A pretty, affectionate, and strong-willed
woman. Miss Love has succeeded despite a troubled
childhood. In addition to charm and a sense of humor,
she possesses a business acumen that wins her an
important role in running Rucker's store. She lives her
life cheerfully and bravely, ignoring or defying the
expectations of the close-minded and suspicious
inhabitants of Cold Sassy.

Mattie Lou Blakeslee Will's grandmother and Rucker's first
wife. Mattie Lou dies three weeks before the novel
begins. Mattie Lou was an excellent gardener and a
devoted caretaker for the sick. The people of Cold
Sassy speak reverently of her, and Rucker never forgets
her companionship and goodwill.

Hoyt Tweedy Will's father. Hoyt is a stern, pious man who loves his family and has a weak spot for modern technology. Although Hoyt is Rucker's son-in-law and a devoted employee, he proves himself capable of standing up to his boss and defending his wife, Mary Willis, when the occasion calls for it.

Mary Willis Tweedy Mattie Lou and Rucker's older daughter. Mary Willis is conventional and nervous, but kind. The death of her mother deeply affects Mary Willis. She mourns for a long time and finds it difficult to forgive her father for remarrying so quickly, which she sees as a betrayal of her mother's memory.

Loma Williams Mary Willis's younger sister. A few years older than her nephew, Will, Loma is a bossy, jealous, and often petulant young woman. She dreams of being a writer or an actress and chafes against her dead-end marriage to the useless Campbell Williams.

Lightfoot McLendon A pretty and studious young girl from the impoverished Mill Town. Lightfoot is the object of Will's affections. Although she marries Hosie Roach, Lightfoot feels affection for Will and parts from him with difficulty.

Campbell Williams Loma's husband. Campbell, called Camp, fails at home and at work. He wants to please but finds himself hampered by his own incompetence. Loma and Rucker criticize him constantly and drive him to despair.

Hosie Roach A twenty-one-year-old boy from Mill Town who attends Will's school despite his advanced age. Although Will considers Hosie his enemy, Hosie shows great promise and the townspeople of Cold Sassy see big things in his future.

Loomis   A black man in Cold Sassy. Loomis is an employee at the general store and the husband of the Tweedys' cook, Queenie. Loomis is a kind and loving man and an excellent preacher.

Miss Effie Belle Tate Rucker's next-door neighbor. Miss Effie Belle Tate loves snooping and gossiping. She embodies the narrow-mindedness, spite, and rumor-mongering that characterize Cold Sassy.

Clayton McAllister A brash, charming, and wealthy rancher from Texas. Clayton's shabby treatment of Miss Love makes her fear love and marriage.

Aunt Carrie An eccentric woman called "aunt" because of her friendship with the Tweedy family. Aunt Carrie's odd mannerisms and theories make her the object of ridicule, but in fact she is a woman of education and poise.

Campbell Junior The baby son of Loma and Camp Williams. Campell Junior is remarkable because of his plumpness.

Queenie   The Tweedys' cook and Loomis's wife. Queenie seems a jovial figure, but in fact she suffers because of the prejudices of white Southerners.

T.R.   Will's dog, named after Theodore Roosevelt.

Mary Toy Tweedy Will's younger sister.

Bluford Jackson Will's deceased friend. Bluford makes a ghostly appearance early in the novel.

ANALYSIS OF MAJOR CHARACTERS

RUCKER BLAKESLEE

Rucker Blakeslee, a grandfather, patriarch, and successful store-owner, is the commanding center of *Cold Sassy Tree*. His imposing physical stature reflects his authority over his family and the ease with which he flouts Cold Sassy's conventions. Not only Rucker's morals but also his wit and prankish tendency stimulate his desire to be a thorn in Cold Sassy's side. He takes particular joy in sham-ing the town's hypocrites. He marries a much younger woman, holds church services in his own home, and puts on a lavish burial for Camp, even though Camp kills himself. Rucker is determined to defy every convention that the rest of the town observes. Cold Sassy grumbles at Rucker's cantankerousness, but Rucker is a fig-ure of integrity for his grandson, Will, and for us. The town is prej-udiced, but Rucker is open-minded. The town clings to outdated rules, but Rucker behaves according to the dictates of his con-science. The town pays lip service to Christianity, but Rucker deci-phers Jesus' words.

Despite—and also because of—Rucker's stubbornness and indi-viduality, he holds a position of authority in Cold Sassy. He owns the general store, which is the hub of the town's business and gossip. He rules, sometimes fiercely, over his obedient daughters and their husbands and children. Because Rucker is an established part of Cold Sassy life, his brashness is easier than it looks. He can safely rail against the status quo, knowing that his power, his will, and his money protect him from the anger his behavior inspires. His rebel-lion commands admiration, but it also sometimes makes scapegoats of Will, Miss Love, and Loomis, who do not have the same power that protects Rucker and makes him invulnerable to criticism.

Rucker becomes more cheerful and easygoing as the novel progresses. During his marriage to Mattie Lou, various difficulties affect his temperament. Although Rucker and Mattie Lou are kind and considerate to each other, the traumas of their marriage make Rucker controlling and stingy. He provides well for his family, but he vents his sadness through miserliness. Under the influence of Miss Love Simpson, however, Rucker begins to exhibit a new generosity and gentleness.

WILL TWEEDY

Many critics have likened Will Tweedy to the boy hero Huckleberry Finn from Mark Twain's novel *The Adventures of Huckleberry Finn*. Like Huck, whose travels in the South help him learn about life, Will's experiences help him understand such complex issues as death, prejudice, and love. Will narrates the novel, and although he is twenty-two when he narrates the events of the story years later, he recaptures the adolescent humor and innocent perspective that allow him to view his grandfather's marriage and the ways of the South with unbiased eyes. This youthful voice keeps the narrative lively, while his adolescent humor lightens the novel's serious examinations of death and morality.

In many ways, Will Tweedy and Rucker Blakeslee are the same man at opposite ends of life's spectrum. Critics frequently describe Will as the mirror image of Rucker in outward appearance and personality. Will and Rucker share a penchant for practical jokes, storytelling, and fighting. Their characters also progress along the same arc—though in different directions—over the course of the story. The novel tells the story of Will's maturation and Rucker's renaissance. Will must learn from his grandfather how to speak his mind and discard the social constraints of Cold Sassy. As Will learns to become defiant and brave, Rucker, whose defiance hardened him, learns to become happy and youthful. Both Will and Rucker move toward the middle point on the spectrum.

MISS LOVE SIMPSON

Miss Love is a spirited young woman capable of speaking her mind, which makes her the perfect companion for the outspoken Rucker. The passages in which she appears bustle with fresh air, sunshine, color, and sexuality, reflecting her vigor. Miss Love also has a vulnerable side, and although she meets Cold Sassy's disapproval with cheery strength, she spends much of her early married life shedding private tears. Miss Love agrees with Rucker's policy of greeting all hardship with boisterous tolerance, but their attitude of cheerful resignation has its flaws. It isn't until Miss Love begins to express her dismay at Cold Sassy's unfriendliness that she becomes happy.

As Rucker and Miss Love's relationship develops and they begin to fall in love with each other, Miss Love reveals the abuse that darkens her past and makes her feel polluted and unworthy of love. Although it pains her to reveal her history, by doing so she deepens her connection to Rucker, ceases to worry that she is hiding a scandalous secret, and eventually becomes truly happy. Her bravery demonstrates that honesty can improve even the worst circumstances. Burns portrays the trauma of Miss Love's childhood as she portrays death—dark, but not hopeless. Miss Love helps Rucker by showing him her ability to convert pain into happiness.

CHARACTER ANALYSIS

THEMES, MOTIFS & SYMBOLS

THEMES

Themes are the fundamental and often universal ideas explored in a literary work.

THE STRUGGLE TO UNDERSTAND DEATH

Death pervades Cold Sassy Tree, a novel that begins with Mattie Lou's death and closes with Rucker's death. The demise of close relatives prompts Will, an adolescent already primed to ponder deep issues, to question the meaning of life and the justness of God. Will himself almost dies, a brush with mortality that intensifies his desire to understand God. He longs to know whether God interferes in the lives of individual people, as Cold Sassy religion maintains.

Rucker acts as Will's spiritual mentor throughout the novel, never lecturing, but sharing with Will his own thoughts on death and God. He holds that God does not interfere to prevent or cause the deaths of individuals and that no amount of prayer will sway him. Rucker thinks that God instituted the general rules guiding death and that humans and animals must live by these rules. Rucker believes that although God will not change the fate of individuals, he will, as Jesus promised, give strength to all who pray for it. Burns portrays death as both a devastatingly sad event and a cause for new life. Because of death, Rucker finds happiness with Miss Love and Loma fulfills her dream of writing plays. By the end of the novel, Will has matured enough to greet death with dignity.

THE DAWNING OF THE MODERN ERA

Modern technology floods the slow, Southern town of Cold Sassy. The novel, which takes place in 1906 and 1907, chronicles a time when people's lives were revolutionized by a host of new conveniences, such as indoor plumbing and toilets, electric light, the automobile, and sound recordings. The novel's first passages introduce such innovative technology as Will comments on the plumbing and telephones that are making their way into every home. The Tweedy family's new car, which fascinates the entire town, is the most visible symbol that Cold Sassy is moving out of the nineteenth century, dominated by railroads, and into twentieth century, dominated by automobiles. Burns portrays technological advances as both positive and negative. When Rucker buys a new record player for Miss Love, the purchase brings the family closer together. In order to expand the railroad lines, however, the tree from which Cold Sassy takes its name must be felled. Even the progressive townspeople cannot help but feel some nostalgia for this symbolic development, which suggests the demise of the town's old-fashioned ways.

THE FIGHT TO OVERCOME SOCIAL CONSTRAINTS

At the smallest whiff of impropriety, Cold Sassy's residents announce their prejudiced disapproval. For the most part, they distrust what is different. The people of Cold Sassy object to outsiders, making Miss Love the focus of their scorn and disapproval because of her Yankee ways and unusual behavior. Cold Sassy also pays strict attention to social status and discriminates against the people of Mill Town, calling them lintheads and looking down on them as poor, uneducated, and dirty.

An integral part of Will's maturation is his struggle to resist the close-mindedness of his hometown. When the novel begins, common sense and innocence make Will question the prejudices that older Cold Sassy residents consider the natural order of things. As the novel progresses, Will must develop the bravery to express his own objections. Will befriends Miss Love and becomes her trusted confidante, despite the fact that the rest of Cold Sassy rejects her, including Will's parents. Will has feelings for Lightfoot, a Mill Town resident, although he stands up for her less successfully than he stands up for Miss Love. Sometimes the omnipresence of Cold Sassy's prejudices saturates Will, and he agrees with provincial beliefs, as he does when he angrily contradicts Miss Love's assertion that racism exists in Cold Sassy. For the most part, however, Will resists mindlessly accepting the beliefs of his elders.

MOTIFS

Motifs are recurring structures, contrasts, or literary devices that can help to develop and inform the text's major themes.

HUMOR AS A COPING MECHANISM

Will often uses humor to deal with the grief and tragedy in his life, telling funny stories to convey or dispel feelings that he does not yet understand. For example, on the way home from the camping trip, Will reacts to the stress of hearing his friends speak disrespectfully about Miss Love by telling a series of tall tales about Loma. To cope with his growing preoccupation with death and the meaning of life, Will tells his friends an anecdote about his great-grandmother's fantastical near-burial. Humor works temporarily, but eventually Will finds that he needs a more lasting way of dealing with his pain. The bond that Will's stories create between him and Loma feels so artificial that he is relieved when they become enemies again. Burns portrays humor as a useful temporary measure but an inadequate substitute for expressing emotion.

FAMILY AS A BURDEN AND A BLESSING

In *Cold Sassy Tree,* families are both a burden and an invaluable support system. Family relationships often consist of power games in which family members try to force one another to behave in certain ways. Rucker's daughters have the power to make his new wife miserable, but Rucker uses his position as head of the family to enforce his decisions. As bitter as these power struggles can be, familial obligations also mean that characters never find themselves alone in times of need. When Camp commits suicide, Rucker stoutly honors his memory, even though Rucker treated Camp badly and resented the fact that his familial bond to Camp forced Rucker to give the lazy boy special treatment. Burns concludes that like all of life's other obstacles, families are a source of grief and anxiety, but that they can also provide succor and foster growth.

LANGUAGE AS A REFLECTION OF CLASS AND PLACE

The language in *Cold Sassy Tree* reflects the regional speech of the period and often reflects a character's class and upbringing. The people of Cold Sassy speak in standard Southern vernacular, and the people of Mill Town speak with a slightly different inflection that reveals their lower social status. Miss Love speaks proper

English because one of her relatives wanted her to sound elegant. Toward the end of the novel, Miss Love inadvertently says "ya'll," a word common in Southern diction and foreign to her proper ways. This utterance signals her gradual acclimation to Cold Sassy's Southern values and traditions.

SYMBOLS

Symbols are objects, characters, figures, or colors used to represent abstract ideas or concepts.

THE COLD SASSY TREE

The Cold Sassy tree gives the novel its title and the town its name, and it symbolizes a number of concepts and characters. The tree stands for Rucker's and Miss Love's strength and composure, and the word *sassy* might refer to their sassy flouting of the town's social conventions. The tree also symbolizes an older era in the town's history. The town takes its name from the trees, and the shrinking sassafras grove parallels the town's bittersweet progress. When settlers first came to Cold Sassy there was a whole grove of sassafras trees. To make room for the new railroad, all but one tree was cut down. At the end of the novel, that last tree is felled so that the tracks can be widened, and the townspeople want to change the name of the town to something more modern. With this eradication of the sassafras trees over time, the town grows more modern and distances itself more from its heritage.

VALENTINE'S DAY

Miss Love Simpson teaches Rucker and Will about love, so it is fitting that her birthday falls on Valentine's Day. Her name also fits her loving, affectionate nature. Valentine's Day comes to symbolize not only Love's sweet nature but also the love shared by Rucker and Miss Love, and the possibility of such love despite social stigmas.

SUMMARY & ANALYSIS

CHAPTERS 1–4

> *Well, good gosh a'mighty! She's dead as she'll ever be,*
> *ain't she? Well, ain't she?*   (See QUOTATIONS, p. 49)

In the year 1914, the novel's narrator, Will Tweedy, recalls the summer of 1906 in Cold Sassy, when he was fourteen years old. His story begins on July 5, 1906, right after Cold Sassy's first Fourth of July celebration since the Civil War, a conflict known in Cold Sassy as the War Between the States. Rucker Blakeslee, Will's grandfather, stops by Will's house and takes a shot of corn whiskey, as he does every day. Rucker's wife, Mattie Lou, always refused to let Rucker keep corn whiskey in the house, and even though Mattie Lou died three weeks earlier, Rucker still keeps his whiskey at Will's house. Rucker asks Will to find his mother, Mary Willis, and Will's aunt, Loma. Will runs to Aunt Loma's to tell her of her father's arrival; she doesn't have a phone. Many people in Cold Sassy, including Will's family, have phones, indoor plumbing, and electricity, but Loma and her husband, Camp, cannot afford such luxuries. Rucker does not have them either, but in his case the problem is stinginess. Once Will, Loma, and Mary Willis have gathered, Rucker announces that he and Mattie Lou had a fine thirty-six years together but that he now plans to marry Miss Love Simpson, the pretty young hat-maker who works at his store. When Loma reminds Rucker that Mattie Lou has been dead only three weeks, he replies, "She's dead as she'll ever be, ain't she?"

SUMMARY: CHAPTER 2

Rucker leaves for the store, and Loma and Mary Willis vent their shock and outrage. Not only is Miss Love young enough to be Rucker's daughter, but she comes from Baltimore, which nearly makes her a Yankee. Loma and Mary worry about what people in the town will say. They think a quick marriage will dishonor their mother's memory. They know they cannot dissuade their father from the marriage, since once Rucker Blakeslee makes up his mind he does what he wants to do.

SUMMARY: CHAPTER 3

Loma leaves with her baby, Campbell Junior, and Mary Willis goes upstairs to rest. Will does not mind his grandfather's impending marriage. Shortly after the Civil War, Rucker lost a hand in a sawmill accident, and Will reasons that Rucker needs someone to look after him now that Mattie Lou is dead. Will begins thinking about how much he hates being in mourning, because it means he can't go fishing, play with his friends, or read the funny papers. Will notes the distinction between being in mourning and actually mourning, and says he does not think his grandmother would want him to stop enjoying life. Will's father, Hoyt, who works at Rucker's store, comes running home with the news that Rucker and Miss Love have just set off to get married. This news comes as a shock, since the family had assumed that Rucker would wait to marry until the end of the yearlong mourning period. Mary Willis weeps and says she thinks that Miss Love will go after the store and the inheritance.

SUMMARY: CHAPTER 4

Will thinks about the irascible old Rucker, a Confederate and a man who still gets into fistfights. Rucker considers Will the son he never had. Will remembers seeing the pretty Miss Love for the first time, shortly after Rucker hired her. Miss Love is fashionable and wears bright colors, nothing like the town's other women, who wear muted tones. She is a suffragette, or advocate for women's right to vote, which makes her unusual in Cold Sassy. She makes fashionable hats and helps the women with their hair. Will thinks Loma is jealous of Miss Love because Loma was the prettiest woman in town until Miss Love moved in. Now Loma is stuck with a husband whom she married just to spite Rucker, who angered her by refusing to let her join an acting troupe. Will thinks about how much he dislikes his bossy aunt.

ANALYSIS: CHAPTERS 1–4

Cold Sassy Tree tells two stories: the story of Will Tweedy and his coming of age, and the story of Rucker and his new love. Will and Rucker share many qualities; in many ways, they are the same figure, shown at opposite ends of life. Townspeople frequently remark on Will's and his grandfather's similar appearance and personality. Will and Rucker both love practical jokes, storytelling, and fighting. Rucker provides the model for what Will might become in his old age. Rucker's integrity informs his actions, including his marriage to Miss Love Simpson. Throughout *Cold Sassy Tree,* Will struggles with the moral consequences of his actions and begins to acquire the convictions that shape Rucker.

Both Will and Rucker question the conformity demanded by the residents of Cold Sassy, although Will simply puzzles over the rules that strike him as illogical while Rucker has grown used to making stubborn, principled objections to those rules. Will resists the trappings of mourning and questions the logic of refraining from pleasure in order to pay tribute to the dead. He begins to understand that one does not need to be in mourning in order to mourn for someone. Rucker, who likely thought just as Will did when he was a boy, does not simply muse about illogical rules, he takes action. For instance, he insists on marrying Love Simpson and ignores the gossip-conscious objections of his daughters. Furthermore, rather than wait and mourn for an amount of time that society arbitrarily considers appropriate, he proceeds with his marriage precisely when he wants to.

Burns shows the damaging close-mindedness of Southern community life. Mary Willis and Loma object to the union of Rucker and Miss Love Simpson partly because they think it shows disrespect toward their dead mother, partly because it makes them worry about their own financial security, but mostly because they fear what the rest of the town will think. They know that people will suggest that Miss Love has her eye on Rucker's money and that Rucker was waiting for Mattie Lou to die so he could marry Miss Love. The people of Cold Sassy welcome tales of impropriety, which allow them to indulge their distrust of everything new and everybody different. Those who have lived in Cold Sassy all their lives feel that they are superior to the poor, blacks, Northerners, and all other outsiders. The townspeople's sour suspicion clashes with Will's innocence, and he is puzzled by the great clamor over his grandfather's new marriage. He does not see why Rucker cannot love both Mattie Lou and Miss Love, or why it is so wrong for Rucker to marry a lovely woman who will help him.

CHAPTERS 5–10

SUMMARY: CHAPTER 5

Will thinks of his late grandmother, Mattie Lou. Mattie Lou was very different than Miss Love, but like Miss Love she was feisty. Mattie Lou was a passionate gardener and was very refined despite her lack of formal education. Rucker began courting her when she was twenty-one and considered an old maid. Will remembers how his grandmother's illness began: one day, Mattie Lou has a stroke and begins to hiccup uncontrollably. Will and Hoyt hurry over to the store to take care of business while Rucker stays with Mattie Lou. Later in the day, the town doctor comes by and tells Hoyt that Mattie Lou cannot be saved.

SUMMARY: CHAPTER 6

Will continues to relate the story of Mattie Lou's death; the townspeople gather to pay their last respects to Mattie Lou, but Rucker won't let anybody see her, not even his daughters. Will enters Mattie Lou's room, finds Rucker crying quietly to himself, and sneaks back out. Later, as Will sits by Mattie Lou's bed, Rucker comes back with a rose to remind Mattie Lou of the day they began courting. Mattie Lou smiles and talks, in slurred speech, of the old days. She then begins to breathe loudly, and Rucker tells Will to pray with him. Rucker prays for God to help him remember that all life and death happens for a reason and asks God to forgive him his sins against Mattie Lou. The next day Mattie Lou is better.

SUMMARY: CHAPTER 7

Will continues that a week later, Mattie Lou begins to deteriorate. As Will sits by her bed, Mattie Lou hallucinates, seeing an old woman crawling on the walls and two men with shovels coming from the graveyard to steal her away. She sees a group of angels, which delights her. That night Mattie Lou dies, and Rucker is heartbroken. Will says that anyone who saw the look on Rucker's face would know that he was not lusting after Miss Love.

SUMMARY: CHAPTER 8

Will continues that Miss Love helps after Mattie Lou's death, cleaning Rucker's house and preparing for the funeral. Miss Love says that Mattie Lou took wonderful care of her when she had the flu and that she would like to help in any way she can. On the morning of Mattie Lou's funeral, Rucker asks Will to help him pick all of Mattie Lou's roses. They attach the flowers to a sack, making a blanket of roses. Rucker will bury Mattie Lou in an expensive, store-bought coffin, which Will points to as evidence that he truly loves her. Will and Rucker go to the fresh grave and line it with the blanket of roses. Rucker tells Will that Mattie Lou once remarked that she would not be afraid of dying if she could be buried in a bed of roses.

SUMMARY: CHAPTER 9
Will continues that Rucker goes back to work the day after the funeral. Rucker behaves coldly to his family and assistants. Miss Effie Bell Tate, Rucker's gossipy neighbor, tells Mary Willis that Rucker sits up late at night.

Back in the present, Will hates being in mourning. He remembers how his younger sister, Mary Toy, got her hair ruined by Aunt Carrie, a bossy eccentric woman with odd ideas who decided to die Mary Toy's hair black because her natural red hair seemed inappropriate for the funeral. Will goes to Rucker's house and remembers Mattie Lou and the stories she used to tell about interesting deaths. It seems unfair that Mattie Lou's death was not that fascinating, since she so enjoyed a grisly story.

SUMMARY: CHAPTER 10
The whole town gathers for the Fourth of July parade. No United States flags appear in Cold Sassy, but the streets are lined with people waving Confederate flags. The parade has several bands, followed by carts full of Confederate army veterans, and the two town suffragettes, Miss Love among them, marching to demand voting rights. Last of all come the younger veterans, who are supposed to charge up Main Street led by Rucker. Because of Mattie Lou's death, however, Rucker declines to be in the parade.

ANALYSIS: CHAPTERS 5–10
We, the town, and Will wonder whether Rucker had feelings for Miss Love before Mattie Lou died. Rucker seems grieved and desperate during Mattie's death, but Will also overhears Rucker beg Mattie forgiveness for his sins. Burns makes us wonder whether Rucker feels repentant because he lusted after Miss Love or even

slept with her, or whether he simply wants forgiveness for the everyday failings of any spouse. Despite his usual stinginess, Rucker has Mattie Lou buried in an expensive coffin, behavior that could signify either grief and love or feelings of guilt. While the town openly wonders if Miss Love and Rucker had feelings for each other before Mattie Lou died, Rucker refuses to acknowledge the debate or defend himself, and he acts standoffish.

Will's lengthy reflection on Mattie Lou's death not only demonstrates that Will is a warm and caring person but allows us to learn about the events around the time of her death. In a town so concerned with propriety, it becomes important for Will, who loves his grandfather deeply, to wipe out any doubts about Rucker's character. In fact, he presents both Rucker's sympathetic side, with his description of the blanket of roses that Rucker makes for Mattie Lou's grave, and Rucker's grumpy side, with his description of how Rucker interrupts customers at his store who try to offer their condolences. Will presents a portrait of Rucker as nothing less than human.

The parade celebrating Southern Independence Day foreshadows the mingling of North and South that occurs with Miss Love and Rucker's imminent marriage. Cold Sassy still lives in the past, and the values of the old Confederacy shape the town's beliefs. The parade honors the Fourth of July, a nationwide holiday dear to the hearts of the Northerners who won independence, but the parade-goers wave Confederate flags and applaud the veterans of the War Between the States, as the Cold Sassy residents call the Civil War. Still, as the parade and the marriage show, both old and new and North and South can live in peace. Miss Love brings the new values of the North to town. She marches in the parade to promote suffrage, a feminist movement that has virtually no support in Cold Sassy. Despite her Yankee behavior, she marries Rucker, one of the Cold Sassy's most prominent citizens and a Civil War veteran.

CHAPTERS 11–16

SUMMARY: CHAPTER 11

Will theorizes that if Rucker can get married, then the mourning period must be over. On the strength of this logic, he decides to go fishing. It is a warm summer day, and Will sets out with his dog, T. R., named after Teddy Roosevelt, who Will saw speak in Atlanta. Will walks by a sassafras tree that was named Cold Sassy by the pioneers who camped near it. The tree used to be just one in an entire grove, but the grove has been cut down to make room for the railroad. Some people want to change the town's name from Cold Sassy to something more dignified and modern.

Loomis, the husband of the Tweedys' cook, Queenie, has told Will that there are fish biting at nearby Blind Tillie Creek. To get there, Will must walk through Mill Town, a desolate settlement of poor hill people who work at the town's cotton mill. As he walks through Mill Town, Will cannot decide whether he hopes to run into Lightfoot McLendon, a pretty girl in his class who lives in Mill Town. Cold Sassy townspeople would frown on Will's feelings for Lightfoot, since "nobody in Mill Town ever amounted to anything." Even though the mill is a key part of the town's progress, Cold Sassy residents look down on its laborers and refer to them as "lintheads." Will hopes that he does not bump into Hosie Roach, another Mill Town resident and an older boy at school who Will fights every week.

While fishing, Will has an impulse to walk across the train trestle, a high, narrow railway bridge running over Blind Tillie Creek.

SUMMARY: CHAPTER 12

T. R. senses danger and runs back down to the creek. Will makes it halfway across the trestle when he hears a train approaching. Will has time to make it to safety, but his fishing pole gets wedged in the rails and he fears that it will derail the train. By the time Will gets the pole free, the train is bearing down upon him. He falls to the ground between the rails and covers his ears. The train roars over Will, covering him with grease and grime, but he survives. His ears feel shattered, and he cannot stand.

SUMMARY: CHAPTER 13

Will looks around dazedly and sees Lightfoot running toward him. He wonders if she is one of the angels his grandmother saw before dying. Lightfoot helps him off the bridge and the train stops. Further along the track, the train stops and the passengers exit and applaud Will. The conductor realizes that another train is coming and the trains will collide if they do not move. T. R. sits on the track, paralyzed with fear, and Will refuses to leave without him. Suddenly, Loomis runs out and retrieves T. R. Loomis, Will, and Lightfoot scramble onto the train along with the other passengers, and they pull away to avoid the other train. Lightfoot has left her bucket of blackberries near the trestle, and Will makes plans with her to retrieve the blackberries the next day. Will is terrified that his parents will be furious when they hear of his near-death experience.

SUMMARY: CHAPTERS 14
Will arrives at home, and Hoyt hugs him for the first time in more than two years. Loma resumes complaining about Rucker's wedding, but Mary Willis stops her and says their father's wedding is not important compared to Will's survival. The whole town is thrilled by the story of Will's miraculous escape. A crowd comes to the Tweedy house to see Will and gossip about Miss Love and Rucker, who have married that day.

SUMMARY: CHAPTER 15
Among the people who come to see Will is Cold Sassy's Methodist preacher, who wonders if Will's escape is a sign that Will is meant for great things. The visitors tell stories of train accidents, most of them gory. One local man who works as a reporter wants to interview Will about his harrowing experience. Suddenly, the group hears Rucker's voice from the veranda.

SUMMARY: CHAPTER 16
Alone in the kitchen, Will tells Rucker about his adventure and is relieved when Rucker does not, as the other visitors do, tell Will to thank God for sparing him or act as if Will's survival were a miracle. Will asks Rucker if God's will saved him from the train. Rucker says Will lived because he had the sense to lie between the tracks and that God can take credit only for giving Will a brain with which to think. Will asks Rucker why Jesus said that if one asks for something one will receive it, even though one doesn't usually get that for which one prays. Rucker says that maybe Jesus was asleep when he said that, maybe people misinterpreted his words, or maybe he never said it at all and the disciples fabricated the promise to entice people to join the church. Will and Rucker go back to the parlor, and Rucker asks everyone to join him in a prayer. He shocks the guests by asking God to bless Mattie Lou, but he moves them by asking God to help Miss Love know that anything good in him comes from Mattie Lou. After the prayer, Mary Willis hugs Miss Love, and all the guests follow her example except for Loma, who storms off in a jealous huff.

ANALYSIS: CHAPTERS 11–16

The prejudices of Cold Sassy extend beyond racism to include class hatred. Cold Sassy residents discriminate against their poor neighbors from Mill Town, ostracizing them and calling them lintheads because they work at the cotton mill. Physical differences distinguish the Cold Sassy residents from the Mill Town residents, who have blonde hair and lint-specked clothes. Like Loomis and Queenie, whose black skin makes them the target of racism, the lintheads' physical differences make them easy to single out. Will becomes uncomfortable when he thinks of his classmates from Mill Town, partly because of their grimy appearance and partly because of his growing awareness of the disparities caused by social class. He feels torn in his feelings for Lightfoot. He is attracted to her common sense, intelligence, and appearance, but he has been conditioned to see her as useless and unworthy of him. Although he senses the unfairness of the stigma against Mill Town residents, Will lacks the confidence to follow his beliefs and openly befriend Lightfoot.

When Will talks to Rucker, he realizes he has an audience eager to hear his story for the story's sake, not for the chance to drool over gossip or make pious remarks. Will's narrow escape from death stimulates his desire to understand life and prompts his curiosity about God and human agency. In Rucker, Will finds someone willing to listen to doubts about God and religions without acting shocked. Only in front of Rucker can Will wonder aloud whether God helped him survive. Doubting that God intervenes in the affairs of men is considered blasphemous in Cold Sassy, where people believe that everything happens according to God's will. After confronting danger and using his own wits to survive, Will feels qualified to wonder whether God saved him or whether he saved himself.

Rucker voices what seems to be the novel's position on God. He says that although God might give people a nudge in one direction or another, people shape their own destinies and God does not interfere in every individual sickness, worry, and event in people's lives. In Rucker's opinion, Will's survival fits with this theory that both divine and human agency influence life; Will survived thanks to his own intelligence, but God gave Will the brain to think with in the first place. Rucker maintains that God makes up the general rules for when people should die, but does not interfere in individual deaths. Rucker thinks that although God never wills any individual's death, he created death to allow for growth and change—the type of growth and change that he undergoes over the course of the novel.

CHAPTERS 17–20

SUMMARY: CHAPTER 17

That night, Will dreams that Lightfoot is calling to him from the railroad tracks. She removes her clothing and Will sees that a train is going to hit her. He tries to call out to her but cannot, and the train shatters her. Will also dreams that he is running from a train, but Loma stands in his way and insists that he call her Aunt Loma or she won't move. Will wakes up and remembers Aunt Loma's twelfth birthday. She and Will, who is only six years her junior, played together like sister and brother until she turned twelve and demanded that Will call her Aunt Loma. Will refused, and Loma broke all of his lead soldiers. Since that day, Will and Loma have hated each other. Will gets furious with Aunt Loma all over again as he remembers that day. He thinks of other people he dislikes, including Hosie Roach and his paternal grandfather. Hoyt's father, Grandpa Tweedy, is a lazy, pious farmer who spends all day sitting on his front porch giving lectures about religion and swatting flies for his pet hen to pick up. Will hates Grandpa Tweedy mostly because Tweedy prohibited Will from fishing on Sundays.

SUMMARY: CHAPTER 18

Will forgets about the date he made with Lightfoot. The newspaper reporter interviews him about his brush with death. Despite everyone's kindness to Miss Love after Rucker's prayer, no one calls on the newlyweds the next day. Mary Willis is livid when she finds that Miss Love is cleaning the house and Rucker wants his daughters to go through Mattie Lou's belongings. Will goes to see if he can help Miss Love around the house. When he arrives, Miss Love has taken a break to play the piano. She is playing boisterous dance music, and her dress has fallen low across her chest. Will, agog, watches Miss Love's breasts bounce for a moment before announcing his presence. To his shock, Will sees that Miss Love has written down the day of her marriage to Rucker in the Bible that belongs to Mattie Lou's family. After looking at Miss Love's arrangement of the house, Will sees that she has her own bedroom and thinks he was right that Rucker married her so she would keep house for him. Rucker arrives, and after lunch Miss Love persuades him to let her give him a haircut and shave off his wild beard. After the haircut, Will can hardly believe how young and distinguished his grandfather looks.

Summary: Chapter 19

How come you married my grandpa?

(See QUOTATIONS, p. 50)

Will and Rucker look even more alike after Miss Love shaves off Rucker's bushy beard, which greatly pleases Will. After Rucker goes back to the store, Will looks around the house. In Miss Love's room, he finds a poster advertising a women's suffrage meeting. Miss Love and Aunt Carrie are the only people in Cold Sassy who openly support women's right to vote. Will suddenly asks Miss Love why she married his grandfather. Hearing himself ask her such a personal question, Will is aghast at his own impudence.

Summary: Chapter 20

Will expects Miss Love to be angry, but she isn't. She explains that her marriage to Rucker is an arrangement, not a real marriage. Rucker needed a housekeeper, so immediately after the Fourth of July parade, he asked Miss Love to marry him. In return, Rucker offered to leave Miss Love the house, the furniture, and two hundred dollars after his death. Will asks Miss Love why she wasn't already married to her former beau, Son Black. Miss Love replies that she never loved Son Black and gave up on marriage after something bad happened to her in Texas. Miss Love does not elaborate on the bad thing that happened to her, but the gossips in Cold Sassy say that she called off her wedding after her fiancé impregnated her best friend. As Will and Miss Love talk, Will sees a well-dressed cowboy walking toward the house.

Analysis: Chapters 17–20

Will's dream in Chapter 17 demonstrates that he is moving toward adulthood. The dream functions as a way for Will to deal with some of the issues he faces as he passes into adolescence. Clearly, he begins a sexual awakening. His fantasy about saving the disrobed Lightfoot shows that he has a newfound subconscious awareness of the female body. Sex and desire begin to permeate his conscious mind as well, as evidenced by the fact that when he visits Miss Love, her heaving bosom and bare knees titillate him. But Will's dream also shows that he is dealing with having to make choices about how he fits into society. Lightfoot is an object of desire for him, while Loma is an object of detestation. In refusing to call Loma his aunt, he effectively rejects the constraints of Cold Sassy society and makes a choice for himself to follow his desires, which include Lightfoot.

Will's blossoming relationship with Miss Love sets him apart from the rest of Cold Sassy. While most townspeople gossip about Miss Love and her marriage to Rucker, Will accepts Miss Love without resenting her presence or condemning her conduct. Will dislikes the gossip and insinuation that entertain the people of Cold Sassy. His description of the rumor mills makes the town sound claustrophobic. Although Will has grown up surrounded by gossip and moral severity, he is young enough to question them. Unhampered by worries about what the town will think, he forms a bond with Miss Love, and she begins to trust him with the intimate details of her marriage to Rucker.

Cold Sassy residents refuse to accept Miss Love because they think that she behaves scandalously, not because her personality offends them. Cold Sassy fears what is different, and Miss Love is exuberantly different. She marches in the Fourth of July parade as a suffragette, a woman dedicated to winning women the right to vote. Her march not only confirms her terrifying feminism, it allies her with Aunt Carrie, the town eccentric and the town's only other suffragette. Then Miss Love marries Rucker, a man more than twice her age. This offends the town because of the disparity in the couple's age, the fact that their marriage comes so soon after Mattie Lou's death, and the perception that Miss Love wants Rucker's money. The townspeople love good gossip, and they also genuinely disapprove of Miss Love's antics, so they spread rumors about her with glee. If Miss Love stopped behaving unconventionally, she might stop their wagging tongues; the townspeople's willingness to hug Miss Love after Rucker's prayer suggests that she might win them over by conforming. Miss Love, however, does not let the town get to her, and she cheerfully stays above the politics of the small town. Miss Love becomes, along with Will and Rucker, a figure of resistance to the status quo. She bears the brunt of the town's hatred for nonconformists, however, since Rucker is protected by his wealth and position, and Will rebels in theory and not in practice.

CHAPTERS 21–27

SUMMARY: CHAPTER 21
The cowboy walks through the door, seizes Miss Love, and begins kissing her passionately. Will is fascinated by the sight, but he becomes alarmed when he sees Rucker's next door neighbor, the elderly Miss Effie Belle Tate, waddling toward the house. Miss Effie Belle Tate is bringing a coconut cake, although Will realizes this gesture is Miss Effie Belle Tate's excuse to investigate the appearance of the cowboy. Will tries to block Miss Effie Belle Tate's view into the house, but she catches a glimpse of the kiss and hurries away to spread the gossip. Miss Love breaks away from the cowboy and bursts into tears. She calls the cowboy, Clayton McAllister, a no-good liar and a rogue. Clayton says he has come to take Miss Love away, and she replies that she is already married.

SUMMARY: CHAPTER 22
Rucker arrives at home. Will speculates that Miss Effie Belle Tate told him what happened, and Will is both excited and worried that Rucker and Clayton will get into a fight. However, Rucker is extremely polite to Clayton, and the two men get along well. As they talk, Will's mind wanders, and he thinks about the religious idea of predestination and wonders whom Miss Love was meant to marry. Rucker invites Clayton to stay the night, but Clayton says he needs to catch the train to Atlanta. He vanishes, leaving his silver-trimmed saddle as a gift for Miss Love. Miss Love worries about the gossip that Miss Effie Bell Tate will spread in Cold Sassy, which is already hostile to her. Rucker asks Miss Love whether she wants to marry Clayton and says that if she does, they can have their marriage annulled.

SUMMARY: CHAPTERS 23
Miss Love says she wants to stay in Cold Sassy and would not want to marry Clayton even if she were not already married. She asks Will to return the saddle to Clayton, and Rucker tries to persuade her to keep it. Miss Love begins to cry, and Rucker, who has no patience for crying, tells her to shut up, which only makes her cry harder. Rucker remembers that one of his country cousins breeds race-horses and has offered to give him one for free. He asks Miss Love if she would like to have a horse, and she brightens at the prospect.

Rucker tells Will to fetch the horse on Monday, and Will proposes that he and his friends combine the errand with a camping trip.

SUMMARY: CHAPTER 24

Will's parents agree to the camping trip, although Mary Willis bursts into tears and asks him not to have too good a time. Later, Hoyt tells Will that Mary Willis has not yet come to terms with Mattie Lou's death. Will assures Miss Love that he will not spread gossip about her and Clayton, but Miss Effie Belle Tate spreads the news all over town. She even pays a visit to Will's house to share the news. Later, Miss Effie Belle Tate tells Will's parents that when Miss Love tried to lead the Methodist congregation in song, everybody remained silent. Miss Love continued playing the church piano anyway, but when she realized the preacher was not going to let her sing any more songs, she left the church.

SUMMARY: CHAPTERS 25

Will and a friend of his hitch a ride with the mailman to Grandpa Tweedy's farm, where they hope to borrow Tweedy's covered wagon for their camping trip. On the way, the mailman tells them how he almost killed his first wife when she cheated on him but that he then thought better of it. Will looks at the farmland around them and says that one day he will become a farmer. Will and his friend receive a cold welcome from Grandpa Tweedy. At dinner, Tweedy frets that there isn't enough room in his plot at the cemetery to bury him and his third wife. His wife jokes that she should be buried next to her first husband, which enrages Tweedy. During dessert, Grandpa Tweedy's mood improves, and he helps Will and his friend hitch the mules to the covered wagon.

SUMMARY: CHAPTER 26

Will and his friends head out for the mountains. Will is thrilled about the trip, but mourns the loss of his friend Bluford Jackson, who died of lockjaw the previous year. Bluford had been planning a camping trip like the one Will is currently enjoying. Problems plague the boys on their trip: bears eat their food, it rains, and Will scares them all with terrifying ghost stories. He tells a true story about his great-grandmother, who was presumed dead and about to be buried when she suddenly sat up in her coffin and began screaming. The boys decide to pick up the horse and head back to town early. On the trip home, the boys tease Will about Miss Love. In his anger, Will reveals that Miss Love and Rucker have separate beds, a fact he had promised to keep secret. Flustered and eager to change the subject, Will makes up stories about Loma. He tells the boys that Loma nursed a pig after her baby was born to keep up her milk supply. He also tells them that on her wedding day, Loma enhanced her flat bosom with inflatable breasts and that during the service one of them leaked with a loud hiss.

SUMMARY: CHAPTER 27
Back in Cold Sassy, Will gives Miss Love the horse, which she names Mr. Beautiful. Will's stories about Loma spread around town and Hoyt whips him as punishment for making up tales. Even Rucker, who usually cannot stand Loma, lectures Will. Rucker tells Will that Miss Love has been removed from her position as piano player at the Methodist church because of her alleged impropriety. In protest, Rucker and Miss Love hold their own service at Rucker's house, with Rucker acting as preacher. Rucker preached about the spirit of Jesus and its power to comfort and heal. Rucker also spoke about the irrelevance of a great deal of Christian doctrine, such as the Resurrection and the fact that Christ's mother was a virgin. Will wonders why no one has scolded him for revealing that Miss Love and Rucker sleep in separate beds, but it turns out that while Will was away, Miss Love told everyone that she and Rucker do not sleep together.

ANALYSIS: CHAPTERS 21–27
Will's sexual awakening continues in these chapters. Breasts increasingly preoccupy him and he pays rapt attention to the kiss between Miss Love and Clayton McAllister. Cold Sassy society relishes the kiss because it makes interesting news, but Will has no interest in turning Clayton's passion into an item of gossip. Rather, the kiss fascinates him because it suggests sexual passion. Will becomes even more interested in Miss Love after seeing her kiss a man. Although Will never expresses his feelings overtly, his fascination with Miss Love's body and with her sexuality indicate that Will has developed a crush on his grandfather's wife. Will's sexual stirrings also inform the lies he makes up about Loma, both of which involve her breasts.

In these chapters Will uses humor to cope with death, relieving the darkness of mortality with outrageous stories. For example, he makes light of death when he tells his friends a true story about his great-grandmother, who was about to be buried when she suddenly sat up in her coffin and began screaming. Will uses storytelling as a way of coping with his emotions and questions, but while his tall tales help him, they also cause him to think more about death. On the camping trip, for example, Will's stories remind him of the death of his friend Bluford, and he begins to question the judgment of a God who would allow a young boy to die.

Throughout *Cold Sassy Tree,* characters use religion both to censure and to rebel. Going to church is not just the celebration of religious belief, it is a ritual that allows for the expression of society's mood. For example, the people at the Methodist church express their disapproval of Miss Love by refusing to join in as she tries to lead the congregation in song. Miss Love manages to ignore the disapproval of individuals, but the disapproval of an organized group of people makes her uncomfortable. Rucker uses religion to rebel, countering the town's rejection of Miss Love by holding his own church service at home. Rucker's sermon reflects his rebellious attitude. He believes that church, like life, should not be a solemn experience and that God exists to provide strength, comfort, and direction, not to restrict. Rucker's relaxed church service and sermon contrast with the practices of Cold Sassy's traditionalists, who believe that God is honored only with stern piety.

Chapters 28–31

Summary: Chapter 28

Mary Willis tells Will how everybody found out about Miss Love's arrangement with Rucker: while Will was away camping, Miss Love went into Rucker's store, where a customer greeted her as Mrs. Blakeslee. Miss Love politely corrected the customer, telling him that she intended to keep her name. This announcement shocked a customer named Mrs. Predmore, who told Miss Love and Rucker that she disapproved of their behavior. Miss Love was outraged by Mrs. Predmore's presumptuousness and announced to the whole store that she and Rucker were married in name only and slept in separate beds. The gossips of Cold Sassy think this arrangement suggests that Miss Love is only after Rucker's money. Mary Willis tells Will that she is beginning to hate Miss Love.

SUMMARY: CHAPTER 29

Loma and her husband, Camp, visit Miss Love in an effort to get Mattie Lou's piano. Miss Love informs them that the piano belongs to her now. She points out that she knows how to play, whereas Loma does not. She does allow Loma to take one of Mattie Lou's mirrors, a large piece with a picture of Saint Cecilia painted on it. Everyone in Cold Sassy has something with Saint Cecilia painted on it. Will says Miss Love has declared war on the family by laying claim to everything in the house.

SUMMARY: CHAPTER 30

Will goes to Rucker's house to help Miss Love train her horse, Mr. Beautiful. Will and Miss Love discuss Queenie, the Tweedys' black cook. Will laughs at the fact that Queenie drinks out of mason jars and eats her food off of old trays. Miss Love tells him that Queenie does so only because her white employers do not want her eating from the same dishes they do, but Will insists that Queenie eats that way by choice. Miss Love's accusations anger Will. He thinks she does not understand life in Georgia, since she is practically a Yankee.

Will finds out that Rucker knows about the kiss between Miss Love and Clayton McAllister. Rucker has two free tickets to New York, and Miss Love asks if Will's parents will be using them. Rucker had planned to send Will's parents to New York to do shopping for the store, but Mary Willis is still mourning her mother and refuses to go. Will assures Miss Love that his mother will not change her mind. Before Will leaves the house, Miss Love thanks him for being her friend.

SUMMARY: CHAPTER 31

Elated by his closeness to Miss Love, Will goes to Loma's house to apologize for the stories he told his friends about her. He arrives to find Loma furious with Camp. It embarrasses Will to see how Camp lets Loma treat him. To Will's shock, Loma is amused by the stories he told. They share a laugh and enjoy each other's company for the whole afternoon. Loma gives Will a journal and encourages Will to write in it every day. Loma herself briefly attended college and once loved the theater, but she no longer has time to write and urges Will to become a writer in her place. Will does not want Loma to plan his life. He wants to be a farmer, even though Rucker expects him to take over the store. Still, Will appreciates Loma's confidence in him and leaves feeling perplexed that he and Loma have gotten along so well.

ANALYSIS: CHAPTERS 28–31

When Miss Love condemns the racism of the some Southern customs, Will initially blames ignorance and Northern snobbishness, but her point of view eventually makes him think about the small racist gestures that are so common as to go unnoticed. Until Miss Love points out the racism of white employers, Will naïvely assumes that Queenie eats from old dishes and trays because she wants to. He is so used to Rucker doing as he pleases and breaking social conventions that he forgets that not everyone in Cold Sassy has the same freedom. Will initially finds Miss Love's opinions peculiar and even arrogant because they are so unfamiliar. By reacting harshly to her views and judging them as ignorant Northern thinking, Will shows that he has partially adopted the close-minded attitudes of his neighbors. Miss Love sets off a series of awakenings in Will. Her sexuality excites his sexual maturation, her marriage to Rucker causes him to question God and society, and her Yankee opinions about life in the South awaken him to the prejudices inherent in his culture.

Loma's husband, Camp, suffers from low self-esteem and worries about what others think of him. At home Loma constantly berates Camp for his ineptitude and at work Rucker berates him for his laziness and lack of initiative. Loma resents Camp because he comes from a poor family and moved up the social ladder when he married her. Rucker and Hoyt are harsh to Camp in an effort to toughen him up. Rucker and Hoyt believe in the absolute value of hard work and believe that buckling down will make Camp a better, stronger person. The constant criticism makes Camp see himself as a disgrace with no hope for redemption. The catty, judgmental town erodes Camp's happiness, and his family makes him feel worthless.

Burns criticizes Rucker and Loma for their heartlessness, but she also suggests that personality can combat the bad behavior of others. Loma yells at Will just as she yells at her husband, telling him he is worthless and trying to take charge of his life. Whereas Camp wilts, however, Will bristles. Will refuses to submit to Loma's will just because she is older than he is, and he refuses even to give much weight to the undeniable truth that she is his aunt. He does not want anyone controlling him, and Loma's attempt at control simply energizes Will to work hard and follow his own heart.

CHAPTERS 32–35

SUMMARY: CHAPTER 32
Will and Hoyt manage to persuade Mary Willis to go on the trip to New York. She has just agreed to go when Rucker arrives and announces that he plans to use the tickets to go to New York with Miss Love. His decision devastates Mary Willis, but Rucker has made up his mind. Rucker embarrasses the family by inviting the entire town to a church service at his house that Sunday. Will is the only person who knows that Rucker is angry at the townspeople for hurting Miss Love with their cruelty and that he is intentionally trying to stir up trouble.

SUMMARY: CHAPTER 33
Rucker asks Loomis to preach at the second church service at the Blakeslee house. Hoyt tells Will that a pretty girl from Mill Town came into Rucker's store and asked Hoyt to tell Will that her father died. Will realizes that the girl must have been Lightfoot McLendon. Hoyt is in an unusually giddy mood and declines to accompany the family to the Presbyterian service. Hoyt never misses these services, and Will and Mary Willis wonder if he could possibly be going to Rucker's service. When they leave church, they realize what Hoyt has been planning. He is waiting outside in a shiny new Cadillac, the first man in Cold Sassy to own a motorcar. Will and Mary Willis get in and drive by Rucker's house. They wave to the surprised crowd leaving Rucker's service but do not stop.

SUMMARY: CHAPTER 34
Some people are jealous of the Tweedys' car, but most people are excited. After practicing driving for a week, Will and Hoyt begin offering rides, and Hoyt pointedly does not offer one to Miss Love. Will and Hoyt ride out to the country to pick up Will's younger sister, Mary Toy, whose hair has recovered from Aunt Carrie's makeover but is still a strange shade of red. Mary Toy asks if she should call Miss Love "Grandma"; Mary Willis tells her to keep calling her Miss Love.

SUMMARY: CHAPTERS 35
Miss Love begins to win friends in Cold Sassy by sending them postcards from New York describing the dresses she has picked out for

them. While he is out driving one day, Will comes upon Lightfoot and takes her for a drive. They park at the cemetery to talk. Lightfoot begins crying because her father is dead, she is too poor to afford a grave marker for him, and her aunt has pulled her out of school. Suddenly, Will takes Lightfoot in his arms and begins kissing her passionately, imitating the way Clayton McAllister kissed Miss Love. They are interrupted by Miss Alice Ann, a nosy woman from Cold Sassy, who tells Lightfoot to keep away from Will in a voice so loud Will thinks it might be God's. As Lightfoot slinks away, Miss Alice Ann lectures Will and tells him she plans to let his parents know what she has seen.

SUMMARY & ANALYSIS

ANALYSIS: CHAPTERS 32–35

Rucker's decision to take Miss Love to New York City instead of letting Mary Willis go complicates the already changing ways in which Will's family members relate to one another. When Rucker was married to Mattie Lou, he stood at the center of the family and acted as a benign dictator. Loma and Mary Willis answered to Rucker because he was their father, and Loma's and Mary Willis's husbands obeyed him because he was their employer. When Rucker chooses Miss Love over Mary Willis for the trip to the city, however, Hoyt decides to go against his father-in-law for the first time in the novel. Instead of standing by his boss's decision, Hoyt challenges Rucker's dominance by buying the town's first automobile. In the old days, Rucker would not have stood for such insubordination, but his new marriage has made him eager to please, and he does nothing to punish Hoyt. Because Rucker has so offended his daughters by remarrying, he can no longer boss them around as he used to. Mary Willis is already so disappointed by her father that his decision to go to New York has no real impact on her.

A number of new technologies come to Cold Sassy over the course of the novel, and these inventions are clear indicators that the town is entering a more modern era. Set in 1906 and 1907, the novel chronicles a time when indoor plumbing, toilets, electric light, recorded sound, and automobiles are beginning to revolutionize the way people live. Rucker's marriage to Miss Love prompts a number of the older townspeople to proclaim that times are changing, and the advent of all this technology shows that, to a certain extent, they are right. For the most part, this change is positive, but the speed with which it comes to Cold Sassy is almost overwhelming. Indeed, before all the residents have even had time to switch over to indoor plumbing, the telephone, and electric power, Hoyt's car has arrived. In later chapters, in fact, a number of the town's traditions are set aside in order to let the new progress continue.

As Rucker and Miss Love experience a romantic awakening during their trip to New York, Will too has a moment of passion when he kisses Lightfoot at the town cemetery. The kiss's cemetery setting is the novel's most direct symbol of the inextricable link between love and death. In the same way that Mattie Lou's death allows Rucker and Miss Love to start a romance, the death of Lightfoot's father also marks the beginning of her romance with Will. Even though Rucker and Will make this progression from death to growth seem natural, it is still very much a taboo in Cold Sassy. Will has not yet broken free of his hometown's traditions and still believes so strongly in the morals of his upbringing that when Miss Alice Ann breaks up the kiss, Will hears her voice as the voice of God. Like Rucker, Will follows his passions, but unlike his grandfather, he is not yet able to ignore the criticisms of his neighbors and parents.

CHAPTERS 36–41

SUMMARY: CHAPTER 36

Will relishes his memories of kissing Lightfoot, but Hoyt is furious when he hears about the kiss and gives Will a harsh whipping. Hoyt also forbids Will to drive the Cadillac for two months. Loma encourages Will to write about the incident. Rucker and Miss Love return from New York and Mary Willis invites them to dinner. While Rucker and Miss Love were in the city, Mary Willis retrieved the Toy family Bible, which chronicles the marriages and deaths of Mattie Lou's family and erased Miss Love's name from it. She orders Will to hide the Bible before Rucker and Miss Love arrive for dinner. Rucker and Miss Love bring gifts for everyone, including driving goggles for Will. The family is surprised to hear that while Rucker was in New York, he decided that he liked automobiles. Rucker tells them that they went dancing in New York City and attended the theater. Aunt Carrie senses the mood of disapproval and says people should do what they like. Silently, Will agrees.

SUMMARY: CHAPTERS 37

Over dinner, it becomes clear that Rucker and Miss Love became close in New York. Rucker says he wants Will to drive him and Miss Love home after dinner. Although Hoyt has forbidden Will to drive, he grudgingly allows the trip. During the drive, Rucker and Miss Love tell Will a secret: they have bought a Pierce sedan, and they intend to sell cars from the general store. To drum up business, they plan on parking their car in front of the store and having Will give driving lessons. Rucker tells Will to keep the plan a secret.

SUMMARY: CHAPTER 38

Miss Love makes up lists of which people might buy which cars, and Will notices her skill at getting the normally stubborn Rucker to do what she wants. Lightfoot stops coming to school, but Will slowly becomes friendly with Hosie Roach, his former enemy. Miss Love begins advertising a big surprise coming to the store. She buys knickknacks for the store to give out and promises free gifts and entertainment for anybody who shows up at the train station on the day the surprise arrives.

SUMMARY: CHAPTER 39

A crowd gathers at the station to see the big surprise, a car. Will drives the new car to the store and a huge crowd follows him all the way. Miss Love does not attend the event, saying she is tired of the gossip that the people of Cold Sassy are always spreading about her. Rucker seems disappointed that she is not there. Though the next day is Sunday, Will gets up before dawn to begin teaching Rucker and Miss Love how to drive. Will and Miss Love play a trick on Rucker by turning the ignition key off just before Rucker tries to crank the engine. At last Rucker gets the engine started and they take off. When they go down a hill, Rucker forgets to hit the brake, and they end up in a ditch. Miss Love seems to have a knack for driving, but when a bee goes down the front of her dress, she crashes the car into a sycamore tree and refuses to drive ever again. The Pierce and the Cadillac attract a huge amount of attention outside the store.

SUMMARY: CHAPTER 40

Will notices that Rucker and Miss Love are treating each other affectionately and wonders if anything happened between them in New York. He drives them to the county fair, where they sell their first car, and they take a long Sunday drive during which Will feels for the first time as if he is intruding on their privacy. While swerving to avoid an overturned car, Will crashes the Pierce into a small creek bed and damages the radiator. He goes for help, and on the way back, sees Rucker and Miss Love kissing.

SUMMARY: CHAPTER 41

> *I'm sayin' I been a-waitin' to hold you in my arms*
> *ever since the day we got married.*
> (See QUOTATIONS, p. 5 1)

Will, Rucker, and Miss Love are too far away from Cold Sassy to get back to town until the car's radiator has been fixed. They spend the night with a local family, where they have one room with a large bed and a small room with two cots. Will and his grandfather share the large bed, but that night, Will hears his grandfather go into Miss Love's room. Will overhears Rucker telling Miss Love that he loves her and wants their marriage to be real. He begins to kiss her. When she stops him, Rucker tells her despondently that he has loved her ever since the first day he saw her. He says he often felt terribly guilty for desiring Miss Love even as Mattie Lou was dying. Rucker also tells Miss Love that he stopped having sex with Mattie Lou after the doctor told him she would die if she had another child.

Miss Love says she could not ever really become Rucker's wife because she has a secret that would make any man hate her. She says this secret was the reason Clayton McAllister broke their engagement. She tells Rucker the secret: when she was twelve and her mother was dying, her father, a miserable drunk, accused her mother of having had an affair. He claimed that Love was not his daughter, and to prove it, he raped Love. Rucker tells Miss Love he loves her nonetheless and that the rape does not matter to him. Miss Love says it does matter, and she sends Rucker away.

The next day, Will almost believes that the whole incident was a dream. He knows that the conversation did happen because on the drive back to Cold Sassy, Rucker sits in the front seat with Will instead of in the back seat next to Miss Love.

ANALYSIS: CHAPTERS 36–41

Miss Love manages to win some acceptance in town by appealing to individual women in Cold Sassy. Her postcards from New York are partially intended to gain business for Rucker's store, but they also work to change Cold Sassy women's low opinion of Miss Love. Even Mary Willis and Loma grudgingly admire Miss Love's post-cards and the descriptions of items she will bring them from New York. The postcards establish a connection between Miss Love and the rest of the women of Cold Sassy, as they find common ground in fashionable clothes. Miss Love's business sense brings her closer to Rucker too. Rucker feels Miss Love's commercial savvy refreshes and challenges him, and he seems renewed every time she reveals a new scheme for the store.

Rucker's confessions about his relationship with Mattie Lou reveal his love for her to be more complicated than it initially seems. Before this confession, we, along with the rest of Cold Sassy, are inclined to think of Rucker and Mattie Lou's life together as a paradise of unconditional love, devotion, and mutual respect. However, their marriage seems less idyllic when Rucker reveals that he and Mattie Lou stopped having sex years before her death. Rucker admits that their lack of intimacy scarred their marriage and resulted in a loss of desire. Rucker truly loved Mattie Lou, but his confessions reveal that like all marriages, his had its flaws and frustrations. Rucker feels great shame because he loved Miss Love since the day they met. This admission complicates our perception of him as a wholly devoted husband and makes his marriage seem realistically bumpy. Even the normally open-minded Will, with whom we align our sympathy, comes to agree with his grandfather's claim that to love two women is a sin.

The revelation that Miss Love's father raped her is a tragic moment in the novel, but it becomes the first step in Miss Love's learning to love again. Miss Love's awful secret goes a long way toward explaining her character. Although she usually seems warm and affectionate, her earlier encounter with Clayton shows that she is hiding some deeply hidden pain. We can also begin to understand why Miss Love so longs for security and safety, and see how she could marry in order to secure herself a home. Rucker and Miss Love's whispered conversation in the bedroom is a painful moment at first, since they each reveal the guilt and shame they have carried. With these revelations, however, comes the potential to start things anew. Rucker and Miss Love's relationship becomes deeper, and the growth of their love brings renewal and healing to both characters.

Rucker shows a spiritual renewal prompted by Miss Love's growing affections, but this rejuvenation is also evident physically. Earlier, Rucker begins to appear more youthful as a result of Miss

SUMMARY & ANALYSIS

Love's giving him a haircut and shaving off his beard. In these chapters, it even seems as if Rucker, normally so stingy and controlling with every aspect of his home, might consider her request to have a bathroom installed in the house. Rucker also exhibits a new love for technology. The fact that he purchases a car becomes an important indicator of his newly energized outlook. We do not even have to look closely at Rucker to realize that he is happier than he has been in a long while.

CHAPTERS 42–46

SUMMARY: CHAPTER 42

Although Rucker feigns cheerfulness even after Miss Love rejects his advances, Will thinks he seems despondent and unusually mean. The owner of a local hotel holds a drawing to determine a progressive new name for the town hotel, and Rucker puts in his own name. Rucker's entry is drawn, and because the hotel owner once cheated him in a land deal, Rucker insists that the hotel be named after him. The man is forced to name his place the Rucker Blakeslee Hotel.

Rucker catches a mysterious illness that requires him to spend all his time at home alone with Miss Love. She is confused about Rucker's illness, since he eats ravenously even though he cannot stop coughing. Rucker and Miss Love begin taking long buggy rides together, and although at first they ride stiffly and silently, after a while they seem utterly absorbed with each other. Loma directs the school Christmas play, and Will plays a practical joke on her by releasing a swarm of rats onto the stage. Rucker and Miss Love laugh hysterically as the town flees the auditorium, but Will feels guilty and apologizes to Loma. Loma tells Will she hates him. Will feels relieved that their relationship is back on hostile ground, since he hates the way Loma treats Camp. Rucker also treats Camp badly, openly stating he should have hired Hosie Roach instead of Camp.

SUMMARY: CHAPTER 43

Camp sends Loma away on a trip to Athens, Georgia, saying he wants to fix the faucet but cannot do it with her standing there watching him fail. The day she leaves, Camp works diligently at the store and seems unusually happy. Camp asks Hoyt to help him fix the faucet, and Hoyt stops by Camp's place after lunch with Will. When Will and his father enter, they hear a gun blast. Camp has covered the floor with an oilcloth, wrapped himself up in it, put a gun in his mouth, and pulled the trigger. In his suicide note, Camp tells Loma that he could no longer bear being such a failure. In a postscript, he says that he fixed the faucet. As Will reads the note, he realizes that despite Camp's shortcomings, he did all he could to make Loma happy. Will hears the faucet dripping and mournfully fixes it for Camp.

Summary: Chapter 44

The whole town buzzes with news of the suicide. Rucker insists on holding a dignified funeral for Camp, even though many in town consider suicide to be an unforgivable sin that does not deserve a funeral. Camp's body is laid out in Rucker's house, and many of the people who come to pay their respects cry and say they could have been nicer to Camp. Rucker insists on burying Camp in the Toy family plot at Mattie Lou's feet. At the funeral, Rucker stares down the minister, who sees Rucker's look and asks the congregation to feel compassion for Camp.

Summary: Chapter 45

Loma and her baby, Campbell Junior, move in with Will's family. At first Loma is bewildered and saddened by Camp's death. She improves rapidly, however, and enjoys the fact that she no longer has to care for Campbell Junior by herself. She spends most of her time writing poems and plays, as she has always wanted to do. On Miss Love's birthday, which falls on Valentine's Day, Miss Love decides to buy herself indoor plumbing, including a bathroom and a kitchen sink. Rucker buys her a record player, and she teaches him to dance. As Will dances with them, he wonders if they still have separate bedrooms. Will is dismayed to learn that Rucker has hired Hosie Roach to replace Camp at the store. Rucker also allows Loma to work at the store as an apprentice milliner. Will bitterly notes that he must work with the two people he hates most in the world, Loma and Hosie.

Summary: Chapter 46

> I better go now, but I ain't never go'n forget you and please don't forget me, Will. (See QUOTATIONS, p. 52)

Will shaves for the first time on his fifteenth birthday and goes to school full of pride. After school, as he hurries to the store, Lightfoot stops him. She says she will no longer be in school because she is getting married and says she intends to keep teaching herself. Lightfoot tells Will she plans to marry Hosie, and she gives Will a buckeye to remember her by. Will sulks at the news of Lightfoot's marriage and hopes something will happen to stop it. He tells us, however, that the one person something *does* happen to is Rucker.

ANALYSIS: CHAPTERS 42–46

Miss Love has such a positive influence on Rucker that he begins to abandon the stinginess that seemed like an integral part of his character. The hardships of his marriage to Mattie Lou soured Rucker's temperament. Worried about his wife's health and unable to sleep with her, Rucker rigidly controlled his life and his money instead of openly venting his frustrations. After his marriage to Miss Love, however, Rucker's happiness changes his behavior. He becomes less careful with his money, buying Miss Love a horse and returning from New York with one of the most expensive automobiles on the market. Eventually he begins spending afternoons away from the store, and even allows Miss Love to have a bathroom installed in his house. Eager to please his lovely new wife, Rucker replaces his stubbornness and stinginess with accommodation and indulgence, and his spirit seems freer than ever before.

Will has grown used to having a special place in his grandfather's heart and worries now that other people command Rucker's attention. Rucker seems to have less time for Will because of Rucker's close relationship with Miss Love, and Will worries that Hosie will eclipse him at the store. Since Hosie can work all day and Will must attend school, Rucker may need Will less than he does now. Will also loses the attention of Lightfoot. In just a short time, Will has lost both his position of favor at the store and the girl he likes. Growing up has, until now, been a pleasurable experience. In this chapter, however, we are also reminded that growing up comes at a price and means that some things must be left behind.

Rucker's willingness to hire Hosie demonstrates again his disregard for the social mores of Cold Sassy and sets him apart from Will, who has yet to break fully with popular opinion. Rucker recognizes Hosie's strong work ethic and ambition and decides to give him a chance. Even when Mary Willis raises objections, Rucker stands by his decision. Will, on the other hand, has not seen Lightfoot since the day at the cemetery. He is upset when she decides to marry Hosie but is too intimidated by society to raise any objections. Throughout the course of the novel, Rucker seems to share a number of similarities to Will, as if they were the same character separated by thirty or so years. Rucker, however, has learned tolerance somewhere along his life's journey, whereas Will does not yet fully have the heart to follow his own convictions.

Throughout the novel, Rucker takes particular satisfaction in shaming people who are petty, and he does so with particular ferocity as he makes arrangements for Camp's funeral. Traditionally, Cold Sassy responds to suicides by ignoring them, but Rucker refuses to let Camp go to his grave unacknowledged. By holding an elaborate funeral and wake for Camp, Rucker forces the townspeople to realize that their cruelty to Camp might have inspired his suicide. Rucker ensures that Camp receives a respectful burial and that the prayer for Camp urges compassion instead of damnation. Ironically, it is perhaps Rucker more than the townspeople who is guilty of treating Camp badly. One could argue that his compassion after Camp's suicide is an attempt to make amends for his mistreatment of Camp and that his anger at the townspeople is an expression of anger at himself. In refusing to allow Cold Sassy to turn its back on Camp, Rucker also refuses to allow himself to ignore his own guilt over Camp's suicide.

CHAPTERS 47–50

SUMMARY: CHAPTER 47

The next week, Rucker works late at the store. As he leaves, two robbers hold him up at gunpoint. They take him into the store and demand to know where the money is kept. Rucker manages to disarm the robbers and forces them to call the police. To prevent the robbers from trying to escape, Rucker fires twice to prove that he is a good shot. The robbers' gun has only two bullets, and knowing the gun is empty, the robbers attack Rucker and beat him brutally.

Summary: Chapter 48

> *They ain't no gar'ntee thet we ain't go'n have no
> troubles and ain't go'n die. But … God'll forgive us
> if'n we ast Him to.* (See QUOTATIONS, p. 53)

Rucker spends a long time in bed recuperating. One day, Will overhears Rucker telling Miss Love that he has thought about Will's
confusion concerning Jesus' unfulfilled promise to give the prayerful what they want. Rucker does not think Jesus promises to grant
prayers for worldly goods. Rather, Rucker says, Jesus promises to
grant qualities like compassion and strength to those who pray for
them. Miss Love says that most people would consider that idea
blasphemous but that it makes perfect sense to her. Rucker and Miss
Love discuss the movement to change Cold Sassy's name to something more modern. A neighboring town, Harmony Grove, has
recently been renamed Commerce, and Rucker says that the new
name makes him cringe. Later that evening, Will hears Miss Love
tell Rucker that her time with him has been the only happy time in
her life. When they kiss, Will realizes that their marriage is now
authentic and, most likely, has been consummated.

Summary: Chapter 49

Rucker catches pneumonia. His condition worsens, and dementia
overtakes him. Rucker begins to think everyone is Mattie Lou, and
he holds conversations with his long-dead father as if they were still
at war together. Miss Love confides to Will that she is pregnant with
Rucker's child. She feels sure the child is a boy, but she cannot tell
Rucker as long as he does not recognize her and as long as his family
surrounds him. Will reflects that Rucker wanted a son more than
anything in the world. Will falls asleep and wakes up when Miss
Love screams. Rucker has died.

Summary: Chapter 50

Rucker leaves a letter behind ordering an immediate and simple
burial. He demands a party instead of a funeral. In his will, Rucker
leaves Miss Love his house and a thousand dollars. He leaves Mary
and Loma their houses, which he owned, and a thousand dollars
apiece. The remaining property goes in equal shares to his daughters
and Miss Love, with the stipulation that any children born after he
dies will receive an equal share. Will knows that his mother and
aunt do not know about Miss Love's pregnancy. Will wonders how

they will take the news that the estate will be split in four rather than in three. Rucker appoints Hoyt manager of the store for as long as he wants the position. The will also says that Will will receive four hundred dollars for college after he works at the store for ten years. Will is annoyed that Rucker thought he could buy Will's services and says it is typical of Rucker to want the last word.

Will expects that Miss Love will leave Cold Sassy, but she decides to stay. She explains to Will that she wants her child to grow up around his natural family. She hopes that Will, who is so much like Rucker, will be like a father to the boy. A month after Rucker's death, Cold Sassy changes its name to Progressive City. The town widens the railroad and cuts down the old sassafras tree to make room for the new tracks. People in town take home pieces of the tree's roots to make sassafras tea. Will says that years later he still has his piece of tree root, along with the newspaper clipping about his escape on the train trestle, a photograph of him, Rucker, and Miss Love, his diploma from an agricultural college, and the buckeye Lightfoot gave him.

ANALYSIS: CHAPTERS 47–50

Despite the deaths that end *Cold Sassy Tree*, hope fills the end of the novel. Will's emotional growth has prepared both him and us for the sorrow of Rucker's passing, and Rucker has died after an impassioned, happy final year. Just as Mattie Lou's death revives Rucker, Rucker's death becomes a source of renewal. Miss Love is pregnant, and her child will be a reminder of the love she and Rucker shared. Rucker leaves not only a physical presence but also a spiritual legacy. Before he dies, he explains what he thinks Jesus meant when he said all prayers will be answered. Throughout the novel, Will and Rucker have been plagued with wondering what "Ask and ye shall receive" truly means, and at the end of the novel, Rucker explains that Jesus meant that anyone who asks for it will receive comfort and strength from God. By providing a satisfactory interpretation of this promise, Rucker leaves Will some peace of mind. Will loses his grandfather and Miss Love loses her husband, but they are both left with the materials necessary for healing.

Burns uses Will's knack for eavesdropping to allow us to witness every important moment in Rucker and Miss Simpson's relationship through the filter of Will's innocence. Will himself is just beginning to discover the nature of love, and his ignorance in such matters mirrors the innocence of Rucker and Miss Love's relationship and prevents us from viewing the marriage with bias. To us, the evolution of Miss Love and Rucker's marriage from an arrangement of convenience to one of affection might seem strange. By letting us see it through Will's eyes, however, Burns is able to establish the innocence and tension in their budding relationship by having it mature at the same pace as Will's understanding of love.

Miss Love's revelation that she is pregnant strengthens the bond between her and Will. In previous chapters, Will eavesdrops in order to learn private information about sex, but now he has grown up a little, and Miss Love chooses to trust him with sensitive information. Will also demonstrates his maturity by his reaction to the news that he will no longer be his grandfather's only surrogate son. Will has struggled to retain his place as his grandfather's favorite, but he reacts with equanimity to the news of Miss Love's pregnancy. He is old enough to feel confident about the place he holds in Rucker's heart.

Cold Sassy Tree does not tidy up all its loose ends; at the end of the novel, no one but Will knows of Miss Love's pregnancy. Burns does not explain whether the town accepts Miss Love's child or whether she has a boy as she thinks she will. This uncertainty suggests that although Will has matured and Cold Sassy has modernized, the story is not yet over, and both Will and the town will continue to grow.

SUMMARY & ANALYSIS

Important Quotations Explained

1. Well, good gosh a'mighty! She's dead as she'll ever be, ain't she? Well, ain't she?

Rucker says these words at the end of Chapter 1 in response to Mary Willis's and Loma's indignant reactions to the news of his second marriage. Rucker's careless response to his daughters' outrage reveals much about his character. Because he feels that he is right, Rucker exercises no tact. Instead of speaking gently to his daughters and explaining the benefits of his remarrying, he speaks roughly of their dead mother, using the approach most certain to offend Mary Willis and Loma. Rucker uses slang to make his point, which contrasts with the refined language that his daughters speak. Rucker responds to their pleas with the colloquial exclamation, "Good gosh a'mighty!" Rucker responds so unfeelingly partly because he feels genuinely frustrated when his daughters do not understand something that seems so clear to him and partly because he does not care enough to avoid shocking them.

2.   How come you married my grandpa?

Will poses this question to Miss Love in Chapter 19, after she has given Rucker a haircut that makes him look much younger. Although the whole town wonders why Miss Love marries Rucker, only Will has the courage to ask her outright. Consequently, he is the first to know the true nature of Rucker's new marriage. This question signals the beginning of Will's friendship with Miss Love. Eventually, Miss Love helps Will understand the world, and this question marks the first time Will turns to her for instruction. It also shows Will's innocence. The townspeople consider themselves too worldly to ask Miss Love this question and would rather make assumptions and dream up scandals than find out the truth. By Cold Sassy's standards, Will's question is an example of bad manners, but Will's ignorance of the ways of the world allows him to act honestly and openly. Will is young enough that he does not care about the town's restrictive rules.

QUOTATIONS

3.   I'm sayin' I love you, dang it! I'm sayin' I want you to
      be my wife! I'm sayin' I been a-waitin' to hold you in
      my arms ever since the day we got married…. No,
      way longer than thet, Lord hep me. Miss Love—Love,
      I been a-waitin' for this minute ever since the day I
      laid eyes on you!

In this quotation from Chapter 41, Rucker reveals his love for Miss Love, changing their relationship. This conversation marks the novel's climax, in which the characters openly discuss the hidden problems that haunt them. The syntax of this quotation reflects the explosiveness and excitement of the moment. Rucker races from exclamation to exclamation, interrupting himself and stammering. Rucker's high emotion shows that he has been wanting to unburden himself of his true feelings for a long time. Rucker speaks honestly. He is not trying to finesse Miss Love or woo her with suave speeches. Rather, Rucker speaks without any artifice, and his raw honesty reveals the strong passion that motivates him.

QUOTATIONS

4. I better go now, but I ain't never go'n forgit you and please don't forgit me, Will.

Lightfoot McLendon speaks these words of farewell to Will at the end of Chapter 46. Her words show the impact of Rucker's kindness to downtrodden people like Loomis and Hosie. Lightfoot makes it clear that without Rucker's help, she and Hosie would not be able to marry. The fact that Rucker hires Hosie means that Rucker has undermined Will's chances with Lightfoot, but we feel little sympathy with Will because, ashamed of Lightfoot, he has neglected her. Lightfoot says she will never forget Will, suggesting she feels genuine affection for him even though she loves Hosie. This turn of events reinforces a lesson for Will. Rucker's relationships with Mattie Lou and Miss Love suggest that people can feel affection for more than one person, and now Lightfoot shows that Will that she feels tenderly toward both him and Hosie.

5.   We can ast for comfort and hope and patience and
     courage . . . and we'll git what we ast for. They ain't
     no gar'ntee thet we ain't go'n have no troubles and
     ain't go'n die. But shore as frogs croak and cows
     bellow, God'll forgive us if'n we ast Him to.

Rucker speaks these words on his deathbed in Chapter 48, revealing the answer to the novel's most persistent question. When Will first encounters death and heartbreak, he wonders how such things can exist in a world created by a just God. As Rucker begins to die, he reveals the answer he has come up with: God does not give material things that the prayerful seek, but he does give strength. Although he does not articulate it until now, this belief motivates Rucker's life. He never avoids confrontation or asks for relief from adversity. Instead, Rucker confronts his problems and realizes that although some trouble is inevitable, trouble does not prevent a happy life. Will understands Rucker's philosophy because Will has gotten past the deaths of loved ones and the failure of his relationship with Lightfoot. Will understands now that such sad occurrences should be recognized, dealt with, and laid to rest, not bemoaned or wished away.

KEY FACTS

FULL TITLE
  Cold Sassy Tree

AUTHOR
  Olive Ann Burns

TYPE OF WORK
  Novel

GENRE
  Coming-of-age tale; love story

LANGUAGE
  English

TIME AND PLACE WRITTEN
  1976–1984, Georgia

DATE OF FIRST PUBLICATION
  1984

PUBLISHER
  Ticknor & Fields

NARRATOR
  Will Tweedy

POINT OF VIEW
  Will narrates in the first person, commenting on the events and people in the story.

TONE
  Will's tone is youthful, exuberant, innocent, and colloquial.

TENSE
  Present

SETTING (TIME)
  1906 and 1907, although Will is telling the story years later, in 1914

SETTING (PLACE)
  Cold Sassy, Georgia

PROTAGONISTS

Rucker Blakeslee and Will Tweedy

MAJOR CONFLICT

Rucker Blakeslee and his new bride, Miss Love Simpson, attempt to live happily and ignore the town's and the Blakeslee family's general condemnation of their union. Will struggles to grow up and maintain his integrity.

RISING ACTION

Rucker announces his marriage to Miss Love; Rucker and Miss Love go to New York City; Will loses Lightfoot to Hosie Roach

CLIMAX

Rucker reveals his love to Miss Love; she reveals that her father raped her

FALLING ACTION

Rucker and Miss Love enjoy their newfound love; Rucker hires Hosie; Will understands the love between Rucker and Miss love

THEMES

The struggle to understand death; the dawning of the modern era; the fight to overcome social constraints

MOTIFS

Humor as a coping mechanism; family as a burden and a blessing; language as a reflection of class and place

SYMBOLS

The Cold Sassy tree; Valentine's Day

FORESHADOWING

In Chapter 46, Will's hope that something bad will happen to Hosie and his comment that it happens to Rucker instead hints at the illness that strikes Rucker and his death shortly thereafter.

KEY FACTS

STUDY QUESTIONS & ESSAY TOPICS

STUDY QUESTIONS

1. *How is Rucker's behavior in his marriage with Mattie Lou different from his behavior in his marriage to Miss Love Simpson?*

During his long marriage to Mattie Lou, Rucker Blakeslee's defining trait was his stubborn miserliness. Although modern conveniences like indoor plumbing, the telephone, and electricity have all come to Cold Sassy by the time Mattie Lou dies, Rucker refused to shoulder the cost of such amenities, even though they would have made Mattie Lou's life much easier. Difficulties placed stress on Rucker's marriage to Mattie Lou. Only two of their many children lived to adulthood, and childbearing became too risky for Mattie Lou. Rucker and Mattie Lou ceased having sex, and Rucker made himself feel useful by throwing himself into the work of providing for his family.

When Rucker marries Miss Love Simpson, his personality begins to change. Stubbornness and miserliness give way to accommodation and indulgence. While Rucker has always been enamored of Miss Love, she marries him out of convenience, but gradually discovers she loves him. Rucker begins to work fewer hours at the store and to loosen his tight grip on money. Rucker discovers that his life can be about more than providing income and food, and he dedicates himself to making himself and his loved ones happy.

2. *How does Rucker's decision to hire Hosie Roach affect
    Will? Is Rucker's decision to hire Hosie generous to Hosie
    or inconsiderate to Will?*

Although Hosie's new job does allow him to marry Lightfoot, Will's
love interest, Rucker does not really harm Will by hiring Hosie.
Although Will is attracted to Lightfoot, he fears his family's reaction
to the knowledge that he likes a lower-class girl. Because of this fear,
Will repeatedly passes on the chance to start a relationship with
Lightfoot. He misses their date to go blackberry-picking and does
not speak to Lightfoot after they kiss. Rucker's decision to hire
Hosie frustrates Will, but in the long run does not deprive Will of an
opportunity he would otherwise seriously pursue. Rucker's decision
does far more good than harm. Rucker offers the struggling young
Hosie the opportunity to make something of himself, and Rucker
does so despite public opinion. Will is not a selfish boy, and he wishes
for Lightfoot the happiness that Hosie's new job brings her.

3. Cold Sassy Tree *concludes with Will listing the objects he has saved from his childhood. How do these objects relate to the story he has just told?*

Each of the objects that Will saves from his childhood is a marker of his steps toward adulthood. The accident on the train trestle stirs up Will's first pressing questions about the link between life and death, and the newspaper article about the incident reminds Will of this first important lesson. The photograph of Will, Rucker, and Miss Love is a token of all the lessons about love that Will learns from that relationship. The root of the sassafras tree reminds Will of old Cold Sassy. The agricultural college diploma reveals that Will has developed strength of character and resisted the easy work of the store to follow his dream of becoming a farmer. Will has defied Rucker's last wishes, and in doing so, acted exactly as Rucker would have. The buckeye stands for Lightfoot, who introduces Will to the joys and pain of love, which enables him to experience life to the fullest.

Suggested Essay Topics

1. Discuss each of the prominent female characters in *Cold Sassy Tree*. Are they relevant to contemporary ideas of womanhood, or can they be read only as figures from a bygone era?

2. Why is Rucker initially so resistant to technology, both inside and outside of the home? What makes him change his mind?

3. At any point, is the marriage of Miss Love or Rucker in serious jeopardy? What causes the problems that threaten the marriage, or what prevents them?

4. Do Will's feelings toward Hosie Roach change over the course of the story? If so, how do they change?

5. How do you think we are supposed to feel about the modernization of Cold Sassy? Overall, is it a change for better or worse?

REVIEW & RESOURCES

QUIZ

1. What causes Rucker death?

    A.   Pneumonia
    B.   A gunshot wound
    C.   Hanging
    D.   An injury sustained in a car accident

2. After whom does Will name his dog?

    A.   Thomas Edison
    B.   Rucker
    C.   Theodore Roosevelt
    D.   Miss Love

3. How old is Aunt Loma?

    A.   Twenty-four
    B.   Twenty
    C.   Thirty-four
    D.   Fifty-one

4. How does Camp commit suicide?

    A.   He hangs himself in the barn
    B.   He swallows rat poison
    C.   He drowns himself in Blind Tillie Creek
    D.   He shoots himself

5. Who sees Miss Love kissing Clayton McAllister?

    A.   Miss Effie Belle Tate
    B.   Miss Ann Boozer
    C.   Aunt Loma
    D.   Hoyt Tweedy

6.   Who directs the school play?

    A.   Miss Effie Belle Tate
    B.   Will
    C.   Aunt Loma
    D.   Aunt Carrie

7.   How is Aunt Carrie related to Will Tweedy?

    A.   She is his sister
    B.   She is his daughter
    C.   She is his cousin
    D.   She is not related at all

8.   Who saves T. R. on the train trestle?

    A.   Will
    B.   Hosie Roach
    C.   Lightfoot
    D.   Loomis

9.   Who is the Tweedys' cook?

    A.   Queenie
    B.   Loomis
    C.   Lightfoot
    D.   Clayton

10.   Who erases Miss Love's name from the Toy family Bible?

    A.   Will
    B.   Aunt Loma
    C.   Mary Willis
    D.   Mattie Lou

11.   What does Miss Love name her racehorse?

    A.   Champion
    B.   Mr. Beautiful
    C.   T. R.
    D.   Rucker

REVIEW & RESOURCES

12. Who goes to New York?

    A. Will and his friends
    B. Aunt Loma and Uncle Camp
    C. Will's parents
    D. Rucker and Miss Love

13. Who raped Miss Love?

    A. Her father
    B. Rucker
    C. Hoyt Tweedy
    D. Will

14. Cold Sassy's first Fourth of July celebration since the Civil War take place in what year?

    A. 1914
    B. 1860
    C. 1906
    D. 1905

15. Who has the first motorcar in Cold Sassy?

    A. Rucker
    B. The Tweedys
    C. The Tates
    D. Miss Love

16. Who was Miss Love's boyfriend before she married Rucker?

    A. Hoyt Tweedy
    B. Will
    C. Campbell Williams
    D. Son Black

17. Who ends up with Mattie Lou's piano?

    A. The Tweedys
    B. Miss Love
    C. The Williamses
    D. The Methodist church

18. What kind of car does Rucker buy?

    A.   A Cadillac

    B.   A Porsche

    C.   A Pierce

    D.   A Model T

19. What does Rucker give Miss Love for her birthday?

    A.   A record player

    B.   A motorcar

    C.   A bathroom

    D.   Electric power

20. When is Miss Love's birthday?

    A.   On the Fourth of July

    B.   On New Year's Day

    C.   On Halloween

    D.   On Valentine's Day

21. Which of Will's friends dies before the novel begins?

    A.   Pink Predmore

    B.   Lee Roy

    C.   Bluford Jackson

    D.   Clayton McAllister

22. According to Miss Love, why does Queenie eat from trays instead of plates?

    A.   She likes big helpings

    B.   Her white employers don't want her to use their dishes

    C.   She likes to bring food home

    D.   Trays are easier to clean

23. What is the new name of Cold Sassy's hotel?

    A.   The Rucker Blakeslee Hotel

    B.   Hotel Bedbug

    C.   The Cold Sassy Inn

    D.   Hotel Prince Edward

REVIEW & RESOURCES

24. Where is Miss Love Simpson from originally?

    A. New York
    B. Baltimore
    C. Texas
    D. Atlanta

25. At the end of the novel, what is the town renamed?

    A. Commerce
    B. Progressive City
    C. Prosperous City
    D. Old Sassy

SUGGESTION FOR FURTHER READING

BEETZ, KIRK H., ed. *Beacham's Encyclopedia of Popular Fiction.* Farmington Hills: The Gale Group, 1996.

REVIEW & RESOURCES

SparkNotes Study Guides: